THE BOWRON LAKES
BRITISH COLUMBIA'S
WILDERNESS CANOE CIRCUIT

THE BOWRON

BRITISH COLUMBIA'S WILDERNESS

LAKES
CANOE CIRCUIT

BY CHRIS HARRIS & JENNY WRIGHT
WITH CONTRIBUTIONS BY

JIM BOYDE & SYD CANNINGS

COUNTRY LIGHT PUBLISHING

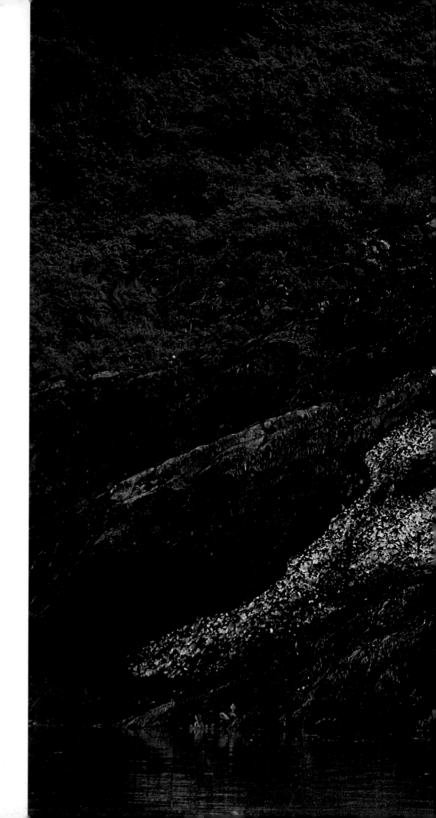

All photography by Chris Harris, except for page 7, by Chic Harris, and pages 5 and 53, by Jenny Wright. Black and white photographs page 82 (HP10126) and 83 (HP10144) courtesy of British Columbia Archives and Record Service.
"Natural History" written by Syd Cannings
"Cultural History" written by Jim Boyde

Edited by Elaine Jones
Map reproduced with permission of British Columbia Ministry of Lands and Parks
Excerpt page 19 from *The Lonely Land* by Sigurd F. Olson. Used by permission of the Canadian Publishers, McClelland & Stewart, Toronto.
Designed by Vic Marks
Typeset by The Typeworks, Vancouver, B.C.
Printed and bound in Hong Kong by Book Art Inc., Toronto

CANADIAN CATALOGUING IN PUBLICATION DATA
Harris, Chris, 1939–
The Bowron Lakes
1. Bowron Lake Provincial Park (B.C.) – Description
and travel. 2. Canoes and canoeing – British Columbia –
Bowron Lake Provincial Park. I. Wright, Jenny, 1961–
II. Title.   FC3815.B69H37 1991 917.11'75 C91-091282-3
F1089.B69H37 1991

PUBLISHED BY
Country Light Publishing
C-333
108 Mile Ranch, B.C.
V0K 2Z0

To order autographed copies of this book and others in the series
"Discovering British Columbia," contact:

Country Light Publishing
C-333
108 Mile Ranch, B.C.
V0K 2Z0
Phone: (604) 791-6631, or Fax: (604) 791-6671

In early spring, travellers will see the remains of huge avalanches that have roared down the many avalanche chutes along Isaac and Lanezi lakes.

DEDICATION

To Chic, whose visual awareness and love for natural things is a constant source of inspiration.

The great horned owl is found throughout British Columbia. Although it is seldom seen by paddlers, the evening silence is often broken by the emphatic hoots of its smaller relative, the barred owl.

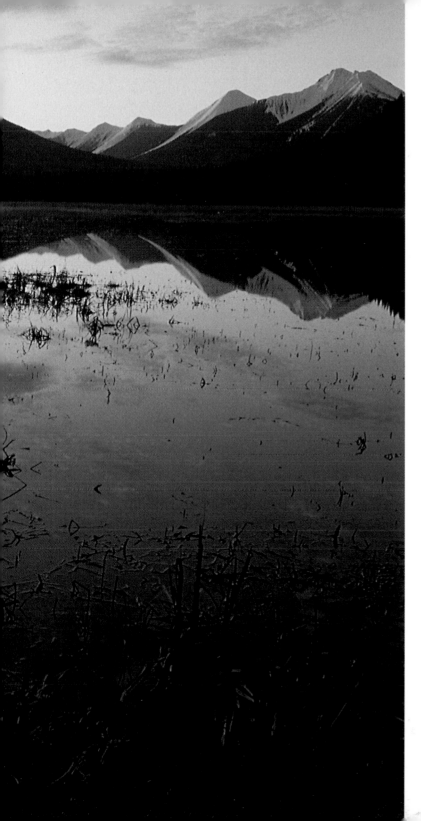

CONTENTS

The marshlands of the upper Bowron River come to life with the first rays of morning light.

BOWRON LAKE PROVINCIAL PARK

Bowron Lake Provincial Park is a magnificent wilderness situated in the Cariboo Mountain Ranges of British Columbia. The park today covers an area of approximately 121,600 hectares. Within its boundaries is a unique circuit of eleven lakes and interconnecting waterways.

This roughly rectangular water system forms a 116-kilometre wilderness canoe circuit unique on the North American continent. The circuit is composed of the major lakes – Bowron, Indianpoint, Isaac, Lanezi, Sandy and Spectacle – as well as small interconnecting lakes, the Cariboo and Bowron rivers, streams and seven portages. No other canoe circuit combines the spectacular mountain scenery, placid lakes, rushing streams and varied wildlife of the Bowron Lake route.

The park is a wildlife sanctuary with a diverse range of habitats, and bird-watching, wildlife-viewing and photography are favourite pastimes of canoeists. Majestic peaks rising to 2,500 metres form the scenic backdrop to the canoe route.

Those canoeing the lakes should be prepared for a wilderness experience and must register at the visitor information centre before setting out and upon leaving. Several campsites, some with old trappers' cabins for emergency use, are located around the circuit.

Since the park was first established in 1961, more than 60,000 people have visited the lakes, underlining the importance of preserving wild areas such as this. We hope that this book will serve as one more voice in the increasing chorus pleading for protection of our remaining wilderness areas – so that our children, like us, may share in an important part of our Canadian cultural heritage, the experiences of our predecessors.

For information on Bowron Lake Provincial Park, write to:

BC Parks
281 First Ave. North
Williams Lake, B.C.,
V2G 7Y7   CANADA

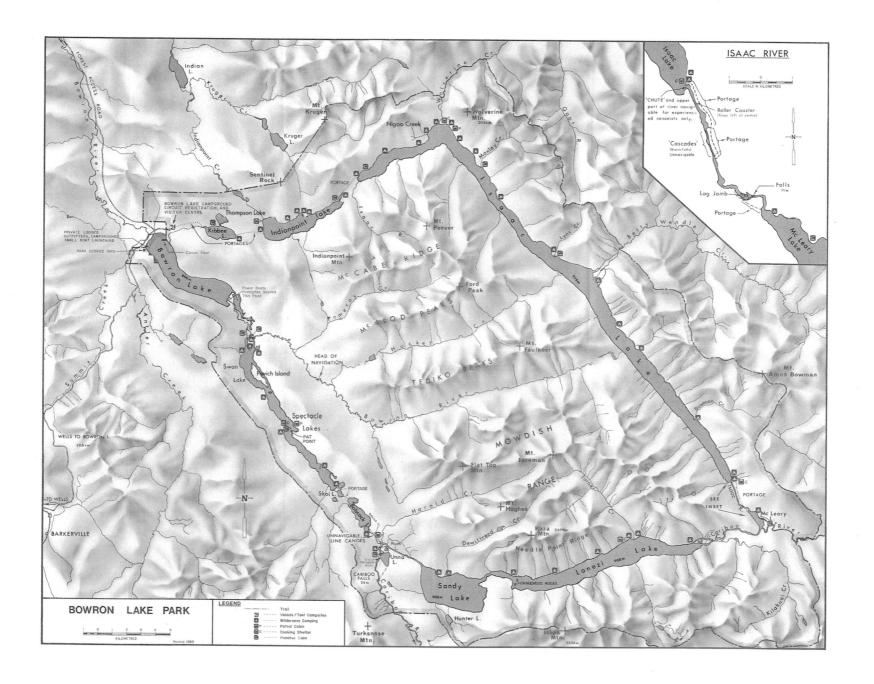

ISAAC RIVER

SCALE IN KILOMETRES

'CHUTE' and upper
part of river navig-
able for experienc-
ed canoeists only.

Portage
Roller Coaster
(Keep left of centre)

Portage

'Cascades'
(Waterfalls)
Unnavigable

Falls
11 m

Log Jamb

Portage

Mc Leary
Lake

Isaac
Lake

Indian
L.

Mt.
Krugen

Kruger
L.

Sentinel
Rock

BOWRON LAKE CAMPGROUND
CIRCUIT REGISTRATION, AND
VISITOR CENTRE

Thompson Lake

Kibbee

PORTAGES

PRIVATE LODGES
OUTFITTERS, CAMPGROUNDS
SMALL BOAT LAUNCHING

PARK SERVICE YARD

Canoe float

Power Boats
Prohibited Beyond
This Point

Bowron Lake

Summit Creek

Anher Creek

Indianpoint Cr.

Nigoo Creek

Indianpoint Lake

Indianpoint
Mtn.

PORTAGE

McCABE RIDGE

Mt.
Peever

Pomeroy Cr.

HEAD OF
NAVIGATION

Swan
Lake

Pavich Island

Spectacle
Lakes

PAT POINT

WELLS TO BOWRON L.
28.8 km

TO WELLS

BARKERVILLE

Skoi L.

PORTAGE

Babcock

UNNAVIGABLE
LINE CANOES

End of Safe
Navigation
Barrier

Rum
L.

Unna
L.

CARIBOO
FALLS
24 m

Turksnose
Mtn.

Hunter L.

Sandy
Lake
908 m

DANGEROUS ROCKS

Ishpa
Mtn.
2530 m

Mc LEOD PEAKS

Ford
Peak

Mt.
Faulkner

Huckey Cr.

TEDIKO PEAKS

Bowron River

Flat Top
Mtn.

Harold Cr.

Mt.
Hughes

Dewittread Cr.

Kaza 2498 m
Mtn.

Needle Point Ridge

Lanezi Lake
908 m

MOWDISH

Mt.
Foreman

RANGE

Isaac Lake

Wolverine Cr.

Wolverine
Mtn.
2056 m

Mosley Cr.

Goal R.

Lynx Cr.

Betty Wendle Cr.

54 m

Bowman Cr.

Mt.
Amos Bowman

SEE
INSET

PORTAGE

Mc Leary

Cariboo River

Turner Cr.

Kibboi Cr.

BOWRON LAKE PARK

KILOMETRES

Revised 1989

LEGEND

	Trail
	Vehicle / Tent Campsites
A	Wilderness Camping
P	Patrol Cabin
C	Cooking Shelter
c	Primitive Cabin

11

THE LAKES

The Bowron Lakes work their magic on all who come to know them. Year after year, from all over the world, paddlers return to renew their acquaintance with this unique chain. Contentment, peace and tranquillity can be found on the lakes, but there is much more: excitement and adventure, feelings of accomplishment and self-reliance, and the romance of connecting with a past that is too often obscured by the rush of daily life. It is a chance to fit into the large slow rhythms of nature, a counterbalance to the pressures and tensions of our modern world.

The joy of paddling is an integral part of these lakes. A canoe is much more than a mode of transportation. Paddlers develop a relationship with their canoe, knowing its strengths and weaknesses, attuning themselves to its response as it slips quietly through the water. They enjoy the artistry of paddling: the dance of water, craft and paddler that relies on the grace of the stroke. This is an atavistic pleasure, a connection to the past — that of native people, who used canoes for thousands of years, and the first explorers, who adopted this ancient technology to cross a vast continent.

The wilderness experience brings all one's senses

Isaac Lake, with the snow-clad Cariboo Mountains in the distance.

alive. There is always the chance of seeing the unexpected — a weasel running along the shore, an eagle hunched on a branch overhanging the lake, a grizzly bear gorging on berries in an avalanche chute just above lake level. There are hazy mornings soft with mist and clear, brilliant days when the mountains seem etched against the sky. At the end of the day, the changing play of light finally fades to a vast sky alight with stars. The smallest images also have the power to entrance — a dewdrop held in suspension at the end of a pine needle, or raindrops on the water, each producing a tiny bubble.

The wilderness can sometimes seem vast and silent, yet it is alive with sound and movement. With dawn come birdsounds, increasing with the light. Sometimes an unseen moose splashes through the marsh or a beaver vigorously chews branches at the water's edge. Lying in your tent you hear the murmur of the trees as the wind rises. Later there is the hiss of the canoe as it parts the water, punctuated by the loud, rattling cry of a kingfisher as it flies from tree to tree in front of you.

An early morning start brings the cool feeling of mist on one's face; at night there is the warmth of the campfire. And there are the smells: the green smell of vast forests of fir, pine and spruce, the pungent smell of woodsmoke after a heavy rain.

Each of these sensory moments encapsulates a memory; together, they recall the intangible rewards of canoeing the lakes. . . and remind us that this is an adventure of the spirit, not just a physical challenge. A

Light reflects off the gunwales of an old cedar and canvas canoe at Unna Lake.

heightened awareness develops when the traveller enters the wilderness, where bears or thunderstorms can suddenly transform a peaceful day. One experiences a pervasive sense of peace — a part of the complex harmony of nature, and the knowledge of weather, wind and water empowers. And there is the companionship of shared work and laughter that binds those who travel the wilderness together.

Great excitement marks the beginning of a canoe trip around the lakes — as well as some anxiety. This is part of the challenge, and the feeling of accomplishment at the end of the circuit is the reward: the knowledge of completing a ten-day journey safely, the friendships forged with those who have shared the experience, the memories that last forever.

We never tire of it. We have spent years exploring the circuit, discovering the many faces of the forest and lakes. When we go in the fall after the snows have disguised the familiar landmarks and the paddlers of summer have disappeared, the feeling of meeting an old friend is there. Each spring we can't wait to dip our paddles into the lakes and travel off on another wilderness adventure.

This book was conceived as a way of expressing our love of the Bowron Lakes. If you have travelled the route, it is tangible evidence of beauty shared. And for those who haven't been there, perhaps it will draw you to the lakes — our favorite parcel of Canadian wilderness.

Chris Harris and Jenny Wright

A camper gets water from Unna Lake at sunrise.

The movement of a canoe is like a tree in the wind. Silence is part of it, and so are the sounds of laughing water, bird songs, and the wind in the trees. It is part of the medium through which it floats; the sky, the water, and the shores. A man is part of his canoe and therefore part of all it knows. The instant he dips his paddle, he flows as it flows, the canoe yielding to his slightest touch and responsive to his every whim and thought . . . there is magic in the feel of a paddle and the movement of a canoe, a magic compounded by distance, adventure, solitude, and peace. The way of a canoe is the way of the wilderness and of a freedom almost forgotten, the open door to waterways of ages past and a way of life with profound and abiding satisfaction.

Sigurd F. Olsen, *The Lonely Land*

LEFT: *Sun breaks through the morning mist on the eastern shore of Bowron Lake, warming paddlers on the last leg of the circuit.*

OVERLEAF: *At the entrance to Kibbee Lake, the beginning of the circuit, there are mixed emotions: the peacefulness imparted by the lakes, excitement and trepidation as the trip gets underway.*

19

Calypso orchid, or fairy slipper, can be seen in the forests on the west side of the circuit. This lovely flower is named for Calypso, in Greek myth the daughter of Atlas, whose name means "to hide." It refers to this orchid's habit of hiding on the mossy floor of shady mature forests.

OPPOSITE: *The pace of canoeing is slow, providing time to absorb images, such as these reflections on the water at the entrance to Skoi Lake.*

ABOVE AND RIGHT: *The aftermath of storms on Isaac Lake can often produce spectacular natural effects.*

OVERLEAF: *A narrow channel winding through a lush sedge marsh is a peaceful entrance into Skoi Lake. This is the smallest of the Bowron lakes: fittingly, its name comes from the Takuli word for infant.*

ABOVE AND RIGHT: *During the fall, the trail between Skoi and Spectacle lakes is ankle-deep in golden birch leaves, making it one of the most memorable portages.*

Some of the most rewarding times are late in the fall, or very early in spring, when there are few other paddlers on the lakes. The remote beauty of Bowron Lake is enhanced by freshly fallen snow on the Tediko Peaks of the park's interior.

Paddlers who take time to climb up one of the avalanche chutes below Mount Kaza may be rewarded with the majestic sight of a mountain goat. This goat, on the ledges overlooking Lanezi Lake, has the thick coat of winter.

OVERLEAF: *Paddlers approach the "chute" at the end of 38 kilometre long Isacc Lake.*

OVERLEAF AND RIGHT: *A beautiful trail at the southern end of Unna Lake leads to twenty-four-metre- high Cariboo Falls. The trail leads through lodgepole pines with an open forest floor carpeted with club mosses, kinnikinnick, twinflowers and snowberry. Past the falls, the Cariboo River descends towards Quesnel Lake, which drains into the Fraser River and eventually enters the Pacific Ocean at Vancouver.*

The deep green waters of 200-metre-deep Isaac Lake reflect an approaching storm, as an angler gets in a few last casts.

A double rainbow signals the end of a storm for paddlers who have temporarily beached their Chestnut wood and canvas canoe on Indianpoint Lake.

OVERLEAF: *The silence of mist-shrouded Unna Lake is often broken only by the muted roar of Cariboo Falls and the call of a loon.*

OPPOSITE: *Many paddlers hope to see large mammals on the circuit, and few are disappointed. One of the most memorable experiences is to canoe quietly through the misty marshes of the upper Bowron River at dawn, as moose graze peacefully among the sedges.*

LEFT: *Red-winged blackbirds are among the first birds to return to the Bowron Lakes each spring. They frequent marshlands and their "onk-a-ree" call can often be heard in the upper Bowron River area.*

A rainbow frames Canada geese as they make their southward migration in the fall.

A solo canoeist searches for the pot of gold on Rum Lake, created by retreating glaciers during the last ice age. "Outwash plains" were created when huge blocks of ice broke off the glaciers and remained for years, covered by gravel outwash. When the ice finally melted, the depressions often formed small lakes, called "kettle" lakes.

Lining the canoe up Babcock Creek is just one of the diverse experiences on the circuit. Amazingly enough, this is the only part of the 116-kilometre circuit that goes against the current. Numerous beaver dams often add to the challenge.

PREVIOUS LEAF: *Canoeists on Sandy Lake.*

This northern flicker, a common woodpecker of the Interior's sunny, open woodlands, is preparing a nest in the sign that directs paddlers from the Cariboo River up Babcock Creek to Babcock Lake. Squirrels and small owls often use the holes that flickers make.

OVERLEAF: *A dark mist rises eerily from Isaac Lake.*

A gentle rain at sunset marks the reflection near the marshlands of the upper Bowron River.

RIGHT: *a magical vista of calm waters and shorelines retreating to far distant mountains seems to draw paddlers forward on Isaac Lake.*

The Isaac River portion of the circuit begins at the "chute", where Isaac Lake empties out through a narrow channel with large boulders on either side. This can be the most exciting part of the trip for some paddlers.

OPPOSITE: *Fed by large snowpacks and glaciers, many waterfalls make their way down to the water's edge from the highest peaks above Isaac and Lanezi lakes.*

This magnificent view is the reward after a 2 kilometre portage from Kibbee Lake..

Fall colours emerge from the Cambrian rock cliffs on the east shore of Spectacle Lake..

Near Nigoo Creek, on the western arm of Isaac Lake, a solo canoeist paddles out to fish in Wolverine Bay. This is one of the best fishing areas on the circuit. In the 1860s, Ken McLeod and his partner, Swamp Angel, travelled a tough twelve hours on foot to sell their catch in Barkerville, where one salmon or twelve rainbow trout would fetch an ounce of gold.

The moment of rounding the corner below Mount Peever and catching sight of the first glaciers is an exhilarating one. They are remnants of the massive river of ice, 2,100 metres thick, that once filled this valley, leaving only the highest peaks untouched. Landmarks such as this white birch leaning out from the shoreline are well-known to returning paddlers, who often greet them as old friends.

Some of the most beautiful, peaceful and memorable times of wilderness canoeing are experienced in the golden hours of dusk.

THE NATURAL HISTORY

***

Soaring peaks and thundering waterfalls; long, clear lakes filled with fish and ringing with the cries of loons; verdant marshes teeming with waterfowl, beaver and moose; lush green forests carpeted with wildflowers and mosses, alive with bears, snowshoe hares and lynx . . . Bowron Lake Park is a wilderness filled with natural beauty and a rich complement of wildlife, both plant and animal. It is remarkable in many ways, all of which can be related to its natural history.

The formation of the Bowron Lake area began over 600 million years ago, when North America's western shore lay roughly along the present Alberta border. Sediments flowing into a shallow, western sea gradually built up and became layered, sedimentary rock.

Most of the rocks making up the mountains inside the chain of lakes are these ancient sedimentary rocks — Precambrian sandstones, mudstones, limestones and conglomerates. Good examples crop out along the Isaac River portage. Somewhat younger Cambrian rocks are exposed along the east side of

Carpets of dogwood (a cousin to the provincial flower, the Pacific dogwood) in bloom can be seen from several campsites.

The yellow-headed blackbird, a robin-sized marsh bird, is a gregarious vocalizer, producing low, hoarse, rasping notes that sound like rusty hinges.

RIGHT: *It is worth paddling below the steep, south-facing slopes at the northwest corner of Lanezi Lake just to see the interesting flowers and lichens on the 400-million-year-old rock outcrops. A keen observer will also notice the transition to lodgepole pine and Douglas fir forest from the darker cedar-hemlock forests to the east.*

Isaac Lake (the limestone north of Betty Wendle Creek and the black phyllite and slate south of it) and along the east shore of Spectacle Lake and the west shore of Indianpoint Lake (limestone). The youngest rocks in the park are from a unit fully 250 million years old; basalts and associated volcanic rocks are exposed in the hills southwest and northwest of Bowron Lake, and conglomerates, limestone, argillite and sandstone of this group crop out on the small island at the north end of Swan Lake.

Beginning about 250 million years ago, the Atlantic Ocean opened up, forcing North America slowly westward. The floor of the Pacific Ocean slid under the continental margin as the continent moved. As dinosaurs roamed the land, a series of island continents (called 'terranes' by geologists) riding on the floor of the Pacific collided with the west coast, bringing the rock foundations of most of British Columbia with them. Among the earliest of these terranes to collide was Quesnellia, a long chunk of land which now makes up much of the central part of the province.

These collisions not only added new land to the continent's edge, but their immense forces pushed against the continental shelf and buckled its sedimentary rock foundations. Fractures and faults formed along lines of weakness, running both parallel and perpendicular to the direction of mountain folding. Water courses entered the fractures and hastened the weathering process. In the Bowron area, this erosion formed the parallelogram of valleys that

OPPOSITE: *In the fall, a brilliant orange fungus called "chicken of the woods" grows in the wet-belt forest on the southeast corner of the circuit.*

make up the present chain of lakes. Gradually the new mountains eroded to a gentler surface, but a few million years ago the region was squeezed once more, forming a new series of mountains. Bowron Park sits astride the boundary between the modern Cariboo Mountains and the eroded plateau surface of the Quesnel Highlands.

The mountains and valleys of Bowron Lake Park acquired their final sculpturing during the ice ages of the last two million years. Four times the snow built up in the mountains and flowed outward in rivers of ice, filling the entire province: only peaks above 2,100 metres elevation escaped. The centre of the glaciation in the province was the Cariboo Mountains, and this area was one of the last regions to become ice-free, about 9,000 years ago.

The icefields and glaciers carved out the sides and floors of valleys, producing the U-shaped valleys typical of glaciated regions. Smaller side valleys (hanging valleys) now enter the main valley some distance above its floor, reminding us that a glacier once filled the valley up to that level. High peaks, such as Kaza and Ishpa, that escaped being completely overrun by the cordilleran ice sheets were carved and plucked by alpine glaciers that left behind spectacular steep-walled cirques, jagged summits and narrow arêtes.

During deglaciation, a glacier or glacial deposits blocked the present drainage of the Cariboo River to the south, and the Isaac Lake system drained out through Indianpoint Lake in the northwest, forming the marshy delta at the east end of Indianpoint Lake. As the dwindling glaciers melted in the valleys, they left behind irregular outwash plains of unsorted

boulders, gravel and sand. Strong winds out of the mountains blew sand and silt through the valleys and formed the loess (glacial silt) and sand deposits in the Sandy and Babcock lakes area. Huge blocks of ice were buried in the plain, and when these finally melted, they left depressions in the valleys; Unna Lake now fills one of these glacial "kettles."

Glaciers do remain in the high, remote sections of the Cariboo Mountains. Their erosive abilities are evident in the milky waters of the Cariboo River and the stunning, azure waters of Lanezi Lake, which are coloured by the silt ground by glaciers from mountain rocks.

The Cariboo Mountains force moisture-laden air masses from the Pacific to rise as they flow eastward, dropping considerable amounts of rain and heavy loads of snow in the winter. Consequently, the mountainous east side of the park is much wetter than the west. This range of precipitation, combined with the rugged topography of the park (which produces its own climatic range — the higher you go, the colder and wetter the climate), results in a wide variety of conditions in a relatively small region. This climatic diversity is reflected in the habitat diversity of Bowron. In fact, the park takes in four of British Columbia's fourteen biogeoclimatic zones — areas that are described in terms of the dominant vegetation on average sites.

This is a rare photograph of a lynx swimming in broad daylight across Indianpoint Lake. The lynx is a secretive and largely nocturnal animal, so spotting one is an exciting event. A proficient climber and swimmer, it usually comes out under cover of darkness to hunt its prey — snowshoe rabbits, rodents, birds and fish.

The sub-boreal spruce zone occurs in the drier northwest (around Kibbee, Indianpoint, Bowron and Swan lakes), where the precipitation is about seventy-five to one hundred centimetres annually. There, open forests of Douglas fir, hybrid spruce, and subalpine fir predominate, with lodgepole pine occurring in areas of recent forest fires. The forest floor is carpeted with such flowers as dwarf dogwood, a miniature version of the provincial flower. In June, these flowers are a vision of white; in August, the scarlet berries are a favourite food of grouse. Common shrubs in this area include black twinberry and highbush cranberry.

The interior cedar-hemlock zone occurs in the wetter east and south valleys of the park (around Isaac, Lanezi, Sandy and Spectacle lakes). Around Isaac Lake, this zone is visible on the lower slopes of the mountainsides, where the pale foliage of the western red cedars clearly marks its boundaries. Douglas firs are no longer seen, replaced by the delicate, droop-tipped western hemlocks. Spruces become less common farther down Isaac Lake and are absent along the eastern half of Lanezi. White birches, indicators of wet, poorly drained soil, lean over the shoreline, and the huge, spiny, maple-shaped leaves of devil's club wave over cascading creeks. This zone is one of contrasts, however — in the narrow, mist-filled canyon of the Isaac River, there is a spectacular moss forest,

OPPOSITE: *The moose is the largest member of the deer family, weighing up to 825 kilograms. This female is browsing among its favourite food, willows. Found throughout the Bowron Lake area, moose have an acute sense of smell and hearing, are strong swimmers, and can run up to fifty-six kilometres per hour.*

but on the sandy, well-drained soils around Unna Lake, an open lodgepole pine forest occurs. The floor of the latter woodland is covered by a beautiful blanket of clubmosses, kinnikinnick, twinflower and snowberry.

The thick forests of the mountainsides along Isaac and Lanezi lakes are sliced open by periodic snow avalanches, which create distinctive tracks down the steep slopes. These chutes are bright green with alder — shrubby trees supple enough to withstand the force of avalanches. Although alders form dense thickets on the chutes, there are also many open areas filled with multitudes of flowers. Gardens of cow parsnip, saxifrages, paintbrush, columbines, buttercups, and many others brighten the steep, rocky mountainside.

The remaining two biogeoclimatic zones in the park are found higher up the mountain slopes. The Engelmann spruce-subalpine fir zone is the mountain equivalent of the great northern spruce forests of Canada. It is characteristic of regions with severe climates — short, cool growing seasons and long, snowy winters. At the lower end of the zone, the forest is normally dense and dark, but approaching timberline it becomes an open parkland, where trees are interspersed with shrubs and a diversity of wildflowers. The highest zone in the park is the alpine tundra zone, the region in which the climate is so harsh that trees cannot grow.

The western portion of the park, which lies at the eastern edge of the Quesnel Highlands, has gentler topography and shallower, more productive lakes than the rugged eastern and southern portions. The lakes are bordered with lush sedge marshes that are homes to many birds and mammals. The tall sedges are often

Bears range throughout the Bowron Lake area, so all food and belongings should be placed in the bear caches that are located at all campsites, portages and trails. The black bear is most active at night, but is seen at all times. It is 75 percent vegetarian, sometimes peeling the bark from trees in search of sap. It is dangerous when injured, when with its young, or when aggravated.

OPPOSITE: *The grizzly, weighing between 200 and 350 kilograms, can be identified by the hump on its shoulder. Its seasonal movements are primarily dictated by food sources: in spring, it dines on fresh vegetation — roots, bulbs, grass and moss — in the avalanche chutes; in the fall it will move to the Bowron River area for spawning sockeye salmon.*

OVERLEAF: *On the upper Bowron River, signs of beaver are plentiful. Trails and canals lead inland and gnawed willow branches along the shore tell of beaver activity. This beaver slipped silently between our canoes, then suddenly broke the morning stillness with a sharp slap of its tail and disappeared. Beaver live fifteen to twenty years and can weight more than twenty-seven kilograms.*

One of the symbols of northern wilderness, the loon is found on all the lakes of the Bowron circuit. Those who hear the haunting call of the loon never forget it. Its call has echoed in the wilderness for 60 million years, a humbling thought for members of a species only 1 or 2 million years old.

mistaken for grasses, but their triangular stems and sharp, angular leaves distinguish them from their distant cousins. Dragonflies love these marshes; in midsummer blue darners swarm over them and emeralds, with their brilliant green eyes, patrol the

OPPOSITE: *Sapsuckers drill neat rows of square holes in birch trees and feed on exuding sap and the insects that are trapped in it. The sapsucker pictured here is a hybrid of the red-naped sapsucker, of the southern interior birch and aspen woodlands, and the red-breasted sapsucker, of coastal and central interior western hemlock forests. The Bowron Lakes lie in a zone of overlap between the two species.*

edges. Small red meadowhawks perch on the sedge leaves and hordes of blue, purple and brown damselflies hunt among them.

Birds are a distinctive part of the Bowron experience. The most obvious species, and perhaps the one that truly symbolizes Bowron's chain of wilderness lakes, is the common loon. Its ringing cries over quiet mountain valleys form one of the long-lasting memories of a Bowron trip. Loons are common on all lakes except Lanezi, whose milky glacial waters are not conducive to the presence of fish. Two other large

In August ,the scarlet berries of the dwarf dogwood, or bunchberry, is a favourite food of grouse. "Running groundpine," a type of club moss common in the Bowron Lake area, is often seen with bunchberry. Club mosses were among the large trees of ancient forests, and their remains make up some of the coal beds of today.

fishing birds often seen in Bowron are the osprey and the bald eagle. The bald eagle sometimes acts more like a pirate, however, chasing the osprey until it gives up its catch.

Along the lakes and rivers, common mergansers raise their young, and joining them on the rushing streams are American dippers, plump grey songbirds

OPPOSITE: *Devil's club fills in the understory in a wet-belt forest, sometimes reaching three metres in height. Its prickly stems and leaves are mildly poisonous and should be avoided.*

that have taken to hunting underwater for insect larvae that crawl among the gravel and rocks. Along the marshy lakeshores, red-necked grebes lay eggs on floating nests tied to the sedges, and common yellowthroats, northern waterthrushes, Lincoln's sparrows and a variety of blackbirds make a cacophony of song. At night, campers might be lucky enough to hear the odd "pumping" call of an American bittern coming from deep within the marsh.

The forests are home to a completely different community of birds. Spruce grouse are commonly

seen along the portages, but many songbirds are heard far more often than they are seen. In the lower coniferous forests, Hammond's flycatchers, ruby-crowned kinglets, winter wrens, chestnut-backed chickadees, Swainson's and varied thrushes, Townsend's and yellow-rumped warblers, dark-eyed juncos, and many others join to produce an impressive chorus on summer mornings. In mixed woodlands, Tennessee and magnolia warblers, America redstarts and warbling vireos sing out.

There are a number of species of owl in the park, but perhaps the most often heard are barred owls. These are large, dark-eyed owls that nest in hollow trees, especially along watercourses. Their surprisingly loud "who cooks for you?" and other associated barks and hoots often shatter the night, startling even the most experienced campers.

Yet another community of birds lives in the high, open country of the alpine and subalpine. Ptarmigan (grouse that turn completely white in winter) are year-round residents high above the lakes. Golden eagles soar and glide over the rocky ridges, looking for grouse, ptarmigan, marmots and groundsquirrels. In the summer, songbirds such as American pipits, rosy finches and horned larks make their home in the rocky, sparse tundra of the high mountains.

Many people canoe the lakes hoping to see large animals, and few are disappointed. Moose are the most common large mammals in the region. Because of the abundant food in the sedge marshes of the

OPPOSITE: *Even a rotting stump has a use in the complex workings of the forest. Here it serves double duty as a base for new growth and a home for some small animal.*

shallower lakes, many stay in the valleys in the summer instead of moving into the high country. One of Bowron's great experiences is to canoe quietly through the misty marshes of the Bowron River at dawn, watching the moose graze peacefully in the sedge. Mule deer are also found throughout the park, but most spend the summer in the parklike woodlands of the subalpine zone. While mountain goats are common in the surrounding mountains, they are quite rare within the chain of lakes. Caribou live both within the chain of lakes and on the outlying mountains, although they are not often seen by lake travellers. The same holds true for wolves, which are more easily seen in winter, when they use the frozen lakes as highways.

Bears, however, are encountered often during the summer. The diversity of food sources in the Bowron area supports a good population of grizzly bears: avalanche areas are good for spring and summer foraging; alpine meadows are rich in roots, greens and groundsquirrels; berries are abundant everywhere; and sockeye salmon ascend the Bowron River in August, providing an end-of-summer feast. Black bears are even more common than grizzlies in the valleys of the park, and encounters are frequent.

Small mammals are abundant in Bowron as well; red squirrels, chipmunks, groundsquirrels, porcupines, muskrats, beavers, snowshoe hares, weasels, mink and marten are all seen regularly. Signs of beaver are every-where along the lakes, but the main delta of the Bow-ron River is especially rich with lodges, trails, stumps and cuttings. Beaver are primarily nocturnal, but can be seen easily at dawn and dusk. Lynx, fox and fisher are also common in the park but are seldom seen.

CULTURAL
HISTORY

S uccessive waves of human occupation have left little mark on the Bowron Lakes, but the history of human endeavour in the area is an interesting one stretching far back into a distant past.

Little is known about the earliest inhabitants of the area, but anthropologists have put together pieces of the puzzle from excavated sites and general theories about the larger movements of groups across and between the continents. It is thought that the first people arrived in North America about 40,000 years ago, crossing from Asia via the Bering land bridge, and gradually spreading as far south as South America. Successive ice ages that covered most of Canada drove the people south; after the retreat of the last great ice sheets, about 10,000 years ago, they were able to move north again. Hunters and gatherers, they gradually formed more specialized local resource-based cultures. The earliest native record in British Columbia is about 10,000 to 12,000 years ago.

The inhabitants of the Bowron Lakes area were a combination of northern Athapaskan, called Carrier,

Half buried in mud, this old scow once belonged to the McCabes, who studied the wildlife of the Bowron Lakes for a decade. It remains hidden in the overgrown brush in Indianpoint Creek below their old homesite.

or Takulli — "people who go upon the water" — and more southern Shuswap cultures. The sparse evidence of these cultures dates from about 2000 years ago. Anthropologists speculate that the two groups adapted to the conditions of the area, coexisting in periods of good relations. Although traditionally hunters of big

permanent year-round habitation in the Bowron Lakes area. Kik-will-ee holes, or pit houses, averaging eight to ten metres in diameter, were located close to the present mouth of Kibbee Creek as it flows into Bowron Lake. The age of these pit houses is not known; built in clay soils, they slumped into Bowron Lake during the

Bowron Lake in the early 1920s.

game, the two species of salmon, spring and sockeye, became the major foods, providing the basis for a stable economy and settlement pattern.

The ready availability of fish resulted in

1964 Alaskan earthquake, unfortunately before they could be carbon dated. Over the years, chipped arrow heads of grey flint have been obtained from fireplace excavations near where the present bridge crosses the

Bowron River at the north end of Bowron Lake and in random places on the west side portages. On Pavich Island, in Swan Lake, near good fishing and trapping grounds, a number of smaller-diameter (one-metre) ground pits have been uncovered. These ground caches could have been used to store salmon for up to

goat, formed regular parts of the Carrier diet and could be obtained with bow and arrows and large snares. Perhaps of equal importance were rabbits, squirrels and other small game that could be snared year-round. Landlocked salmon, whitefish, lake trout, suckers and ling cod were also caught seasonally. Canoes, both

The Indianpoint to Isaac Lake portage. Photographs by J.D. Babcock.

a year. Salmon were caught in weirs and basket traps. Nets were also used — for fishing, for trapping beaver under the ice, and for gathering grebes when in moult.

Big game animals, such as caribou, elk, deer and

dugout and spruce bark, were used extensively.

It wasn't until 1805, when Simon Fraser, exploring for the North West Company, established Fort McCleod on the portage to the Fraser River from the

Joe and Betty Wendle were some of the first conservationists in the Bowron Lakes area, and their cabin on the upper Bowron River is the oldest remaining structure on the lakes.

Peace River, that there was continuous European contact with Interior Carriers, including those in the Bowron Lakes region. Earlier European trade influence from the coast, and Alexander Mackenzie's voyage to the Pacific in 1793, were more casual contacts.

During the early 1860s the Cariboo gold rush moved north, bringing rapid settlement. As the trickle of Europeans increased in the 1860s, the town of Barkerville was established. One of its earlier residents was John Bowron. Drawn by the lure of the west, he left his study of law in Ohio to join the Overlanders of '62, a group heading for the goldfields of the Cariboo. From 1863 to 1906 he lived in Barkerville, holding

posts ranging from postmaster to fire warden, government agent and finally gold commissioner. To commemorate him, the lake known as Bear Lake was renamed Bowron in 1914.

Inevitably, European contact brought problems and disease for the native population. In the early '60s, the first two trappers known to have lived on the Bowron Lakes, Ken McLeod and his partner Neil Wilson, known as 'Swampy' or 'Swamp Angel,' found a lone woman — the single survivor of a scourge of small pox that had recently wiped out her entire tribe. The remains of the rest of the tribe, numbering several hundred people, were at the north end of Pavich

Island in Swan Lake. The plague, she told the trappers, was a punishment for the murder of a white man who had come down Antler Creek. By the late 1860s, there were no permanent native residents at the lakes, although it was used seasonally.

McLeod and Swamp Angel lived on the Bowron Lakes for forty years. They trapped and fished, travelling to gold towns like Barkerville — in summer, an arduous twelve-hour journey by foot — to sell their produce. It was almost as valuable as gold and people were reported to line up when the news went out that the two men were in town. When they weren't fishing they were partners with George Isaac, a logger and sawyer in the early years, for whom the park's longest lake is named.

The Bowron Lakes area had plentiful fish and wildlife and were used extensively as a food resource, and later as a hunting preserve of rich Americans. One of the area's most fascinating characters was Frank Kibbee, a marksman of note and teller of tall tales who lived and trapped there with his companion, Emma. Moose began appearing in the area around this time (1906-10) and Kibbee made a good living guiding hunting parties. Stories about Kibbee abound. One details an incident where Kibbee and a wealthy American were tracking a grizzly wounded from a trap. They decided to separate and Kibbee heard shots. When he came to within hailing distance of the American, he found that he had been shooting at grouse, which prompted Kibbee to expound, in a highly embroidered style, that when hunting grizzly, one does not shoot at grouse. Meanwhile, the grizzly was charging down the ridge at them. Kibbee, armed with a handgun, shot the bear in the neck, but it

continued the charge. The American handed his shotgun to Kibbee, who calmly waited until the bear was within six metres before firing, only to discover that the American had forgotten to reload after firing at the grouse. Kibbee was severely mauled and was not expected to live. However, he survived to shoot himself in the knee a short time later. He married a mail-order bride, an English girl of Spanish descent named Juanita Anita, and built the first home on the lakes. Kibbee Lake was named for him in 1921.

In 1912, Frank Kibbee guided Joe Wendle around the lakes chain and it formed the basis for a lifelong quest to have the area set aside as a park. The Wendles spent twenty years as guides. They built three lodges (the first two burned down), established cabins and brought a new awareness of conservation to the use of wildlife in the area. Joe Wendle was an avid fisherman and the Bowron River above Bowron Lake was one of his favourite fishing holes. The cabin he built there in 1926 still stands, the oldest remaining cabin on the circuit, witness to the yearly salmon runs, moose calves, bird migrations, silent sunsets and icebound winters that he loved.

Although he was a renowned guide, Kibbee was well aware of diminishing wildlife and conservation ethics. He, along with Joe and Betty Wendle, J.P. Babcock (B.C. Fish Commissioner and a regular visitor from Victoria), and Chief Justice Hunter of the B.C. Supreme Court were successful in having the interior of the lake chain set aside as a game reserve in 1925. Kibbee became the first long-term game warden.

OVERLEAF: *The view from Wendle's cabin, looking eastward toward the park's interior.*

Thomas McCabe and his wife, Eleanor, heard about the Bowron Lakes while cruising the B.C. coast. In 1924, they built a fine log home on Indianpoint Lake and began a systematic study of the natural life of the area. At this time local game and fish guides were using Bowron Lake as a thoroughfare to the entire west side of the chain, and overhunting had become a serious problem. The McCabes joined the growing chorus of Bowron Lakes conservationists who were seeking park status for the area. They remained until 1934, when Thomas McCabe moved to Berkley, California, to lecture in ornithology. Some flowers unusual to the area, remnants of Eleanor's garden, and the stone chimney of their house are all that remain of their years at the lakes.

Development continued in the Bowron area, with several people granted lots of Crown land on the lakes. By 1933, two lodges, Wendle's and Youngs' (both of which have lasted as landmarks on the lakes), and several cabins had been built on the northwest shore of Bowron Lake. Dances held at the lodges attracted people from as far away as Quesnel and Prince George, as well as Barkerville and Wells. In 1935, Wendle's Lodge was sold to Bill McKitrick, whose family still own and operate it under the name Bowron Lake Lodge.

The log building that perches on the rise of land overlooking Bowron Lake and the interior park mountains was built by Grover and Elsie Youngs in 1933 and was known as the Cariboo Hunting and Fishing Lodge. The axework on this lodge is superb. Logs for the building were cut from the local forest of Engelmann spruce, and the furniture, styled after that originally made by Wendle for his lodge, was fashioned from Bowron Lake birch trees. Shakes for the roof came from the massive stands of red cedar that grew on the north shore of Sandy Lake, and getting the cedar to the building site was no easy task. The giant trees were felled and bucked, then dragged to the lakeshore, where rafts of cedar bolts were assembled. Then the long journey began. The bolts were rafted down Sandy Lake and the Cariboo River to the Babcock portage, rafted across Babcock Lake, portaged to Skoi Lake, rafted across Skoi and portaged to Spectacle Lake. From here the rafts were motored eleven kilometres to the beach below the worksite on Bowron Lake, hauled up the steep slope, then finally split into shakes. Although the cedar shake roof has now been replaced by metal, a stand of the magnificent giant cedars still graces the south-facing slopes of Sandy Lake. Doddie and Fred Becker assumed ownership of the lodge in 1969 and renamed it Becker's Lodge, by which it is known today.

Shortly after making a first trip around the lakes with his wife, Lorna Boyd, in 1935, Old Freddie Becker (no connection with Becker's Lodge) built his first cabin on McLeary Lake. His family lived in Wells, and Becker spent the winter months on his isolated traplines around the lakes. On the way out to McCleary Lake, Freddie would stop by Ole Nelson's

OPPOSITE: *The McCabe's homesite on Indianpoint Creek was a log building with French windows and hand-carved window shutters. Thomas and Eleanor were naturalists who banded birds and kept meticulous records, all of which formed part of an already large library of books in their cozy home. All that remains today are some flowers unusual to the area, remnants of Eleanor's garden, and a stone chimney.*

place at Wolverine Bay and they would often net kokanee spawning in the freshwater seepages at the head of the bay. Dolly Varden and lake trout were easily caught at this time as they came inshore to dine on the kokanee. After a few days of smoking fish, they would make plans to rendezvous again in late November at Betty Wendle Creek, where Ole had another cabin, and Becker would be off down Isaac.

The stories told by trappers and guides all share a common feeling — that their Bowron Lakes experiences were almost magical, a highlight of their lives. It was also a life of some hardship and danger. Old Freddie Becker told of the time he decided to snowshoe back down to McCleary Lake from his line cabin on the Upper Cariboo. It was a crisp moonlit night, about 20 below Fahrenheit, and so clear he could hear the train whistle in Tete Jaune Cache, a hundred kilometres over the mountains. Old Freddie started downriver with his Irish wolfhound, Pupper. Keeping a good pace, he became aware that Pupper was warning him to stop. Not a metre away was a black, silently flowing, open stretch of water. Several more steps and his life would have ended. Old Freddie sat with his hand on his dog's head and said a silent prayer; from that day on he always carried a pole when snowshoeing on ice.

Over the years, recreational use of the lakes broadened. In the 1940s, the Wells Rod and Reel Club was established and began to enhance recreational fishing on the lakes. Several cabins were established with adjoining campsites. The most dramatic changes came in 1947, when a proposal was made by the Forest Service to make the Bowron Lake Game Preserve a park. The plans had a close call when the B.C. Power Commission placed a reserve on the area for the purpose of studying hydroelectric potential at Isaac and Cariboo falls. Isaac Falls was quickly ruled out, but studies of Cariboo Falls included mapping the area for flood levels. Fortunately, the hydroelectric project proved to be uneconomical, saving one of the world's premier wilderness canoeing circuits from oblivion.

In 1956, 120,318 hectares of the reserve was set aside for purely recreational purposes. In 1961, the recreational reserve was purchased by government and designated a park, thus ensuring that the Bowron Lakes will be enjoyed by generations to come. Another 2,488 hectares were added in 1970. Unfortunately, in its zeal to protect the "wilderness," much of the historic value was lost when the old cabins, including the McCabe lodge with all its books and records of local wildlife, were burned down. The sites that remain, reminders of the tough, brave people who came before, add immeasurably to the experience of today's wilderness adventurers.

In 1935, Old Freddie Becker built his first cabin on McLeary Lake. He would come to the cabin as the first snows fell to begin his long four or five months on his isolated traplines. This is one of his cabins that still remains.

OVERLEAF: *On his return to Barkerville, Freddie Becker would drop in to Ole Nelson's place at the base of Wolverine Mountain, below the avalanche chutes visible in the photograph. Here they would exchange stories of their winter sojourn before Becker returned to civilization.*

ACKNOWLEDGEMENTS

Our joy in creating this book has been the sharing of information and enthusiasm with many close friends. We are especially grateful for the contributions of the natural and cultural history sections by our friends Syd Cannings and Jim Boyde. This information is so vital to a meaningful canoe journey around the lakes; for their expert knowledge in these areas we are very thankful.

We also wish to thank Betty and Ken Cairns, Mike and Darlene Calyniuk, Ruth McLaren, Dave Milligan, Bob Herger, Cindy Carscadden, Gordon Milne and Tom Ellison for their valuable assistance and encouragement. Thanks also to our good friend Dean Hull, who has paddled the circuit many times and was always there with ideas and encouragement in support of our efforts to create this book. Pat Hancock deserves special thanks for providing us with a home-away-from-home while we worked on the book. Thanks also to Gerry and Marie Weldon, who so generously provided a home base in Quesnel, from which we have launched all our Bowron Lake canoe expeditions.

We also deeply appreciate the help of our editor, Elaine Jones. Her insight, understanding and knowledge of book publishing helped to make our first book a reality.

Chris Harris and Jenny Wright

As a photographer, I continue to be inspired by my father, Chic Harris, and my sister and her husband, Jane and Tony O'Malley — artists who have shown me the beauty in familiar things.

Chris Harris

Sunset is often a time to reflect on the trip - the joys and challenges, companionship and the sense of being a part of nature.

"DISCOVER BRITISH COLUMBIA"®
Book, Card & Print Series

Through the *"Discover British Columbia"®* book, card and print series, Chris presents the opportunity to explore or revisit unique areas of BC, to marvel at and reflect upon their natural beauty, and to honor and appreciate the necessity of preserving this heritage.

The following four books have been published by Country Light Publishing and Chris Harris Photography. You can purchase these from your local bookstore or order autographed copies by contacting:

COUNTRY LIGHT PUBLISHING
Box 333–108 Mile Ranch
British Columbia, Canada, V0K 2Z0
Tel: 250-791-6631   Fax: 250-791-6671
1-800-946-6622
e-mail: harrisc@netshop.net

THE BOWRON LAKES

British Columbia's Wilderness Canoe Circuit is a photographic portrayal of "one of the top 10 canoe trips in the world" (*Outside Magazine*). This unique natural circuit of lakes and interconnecting waterways is situated in a wildlife sanctuary amidst the snow-capped Cariboo Mountains.

ISBN 0-9695235-0-5 $24.95 (soft cover)

CARIBOO COUNTRY

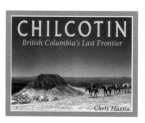

British Columbia's Spirit of the West is a photographic portrayal of the region's western heritage. It's a land which offers a magic and beauty stunning in its diversity.

ISBN 0-9695235-3-x $26.95 (soft cover)
ISBN 0-9695235-4-8 $36.95 (hard cover)

BC RAIL

British Columbia's Great Train Adventure captures the sense of exploration, excitement and romance along a 1,000-mile journey which encompasses some of the most spectacular and varied scenery in British Columbia.

ISBN 0-9695235-1-3 $24.95 (soft cover)
ISBN 0-9695235-2-1 $34.95 (hard cover)

CHILCOTIN

British Columbia's Last Frontier. Born out of volcanic activity and weathered by erosion, the physical and human landscapes of the Chilcotin Plateau and Bella Coola Valley have a color and composition unparalleled anywhere in BC. This photographic portrayal captures that energy and enchantment.

ISBN 0-9695235-7-2 $26.95 (soft cover)
ISBN 0-9695235-6-4 $36.95 (hard cover)